◆ ◆ *Round for One Voice*

♦ ♦*Round for One Voice*

poems by

Dan Jaffe

The University of Arkansas Press
Fayetteville ♦ London ♦ 1988

Copyright © 1988 by Dan Jaffe
All rights reserved
Manufactured in the United States
92 91 90 89 88   5 4 3 2 1

Designer: Chiquita Babb
Typeface: Linotron 202 Century Old Style
Typesetter: G&S Typesetters, Inc.
Printer: McNaughton & Gunn, Inc.
Binder: John H. Dekker & Sons, Inc.

Acknowledgments appear on page 63.

The paper used in this publication meets the minimum requirements of the American National Standard for Permanence of Paper for Printed Library Materials Z39.48-1984. ∞

Library of Congress Cataloging-in-Publication Data
Jaffe, Dan.
   Round for one voice.
I. Title.
PS3560.A3R68   1988   811'.54   87-35813
ISBN 1-55728-032-0 (alk. paper)
ISBN 1-55728-033-9 (pbk. : alk. paper)

*For
Robin Gale*

Contents

The Forecast   *3*
Forty-four Ladies in a Golden Age Bus   *4*
Weather Watch   *5*
After Midnight   *6*
Addie Parker's Blues   *7*
Black Woman, Enroute   *9*
Disillusionment at Dawn   *10*
P.S.   *11*
At Dinner They Punned   *12*
New Year's Eve   *13*
On U.S. 1   *14*
Ninth Street Bar, Seen Through the Glass   *15*
The Body of This World   *16*
Biography   *17*
To Calypso: Five-Week-Old German Shepherd   *18*
A Matter of Balance   *19*
Excursion   *20*
View from the Trestle   *21*
Lady in Waiting   *22*
The Soviet Flu   *24*
Standing Before a Lit Menorah   *25*
Learning About Easter and Passover   *26*
Poem for a Bar Mitzvah   *28*
Survivor   *30*
Yahrzeit   *32*
The Holy Days   *33*

The Tragedy of Shylock   *35*
Wedding at the Western Wall   *42*
Things Always Need Repairing   *43*
A Monument of Feeling Stones   *44*
Leaving Murray Hall, Elizabeth, N.J.   *45*
Menorah Hospital, May 347 1971, 9:55 a.m.   *47*
Waiting for You to Reappear in the House We Never Left   *48*
The Year We Moved from Currey Head   *51*
The Middle Aged Man Looks Out into the Gulf   *55*
Breathing In   *57*
They Would Be My Poems   *58*
Whitman on a Scaffold   *59*
Round for One Voice   *62*

♦ ♦ Round For One Voice

◆ *The Forecast*

Perhaps our age has driven us indoors.
We sprawl in the semi-darkness, dreaming sometimes
Of a vague world spinning in the wind.
But we have snapped our locks, pulled down our shades,
Taken all precautions. We shall not be disturbed.
If the earth shakes, it will be on a screen;
And if the prairie wind spills down our streets
And covers us with leaves, the weatherman will tell us.

Forty-four Ladies in a Golden Age Bus

Forty-four ladies in a Golden Age bus
Squint out windows at the passing day,
Drown out horsepower with morning chatter.
This is the tour that rolls over the years,
That turns the arterial buzz in your head
To a highway hum. While the driver quips,
They giggle like girls on the way to a dance.
What they need they say is a barrel of cider.
It keeps you going on a trip like this.
What they need they say is a twilight romp
With forty-four drivers who know how.
But they wouldn't take a bag full of money
For the times that they already had.
Forty-four ladies in a Golden Age bus,
Pockets plump with Ozark diamonds,
Satchels stuffed with gift shop china,
Lean back against their seats and sigh,
As their journey ends, grow still as stars.

• *Weather Watch*

Along the banks of the Little Blue
maples wrestle in the wind
under an introspective sky.

A weasel wanders warily through;
a deer accuses the midnight moon,
and the philosophic grasses sigh.

Slowly a pebble turns in its bed;
a squirrel assays the year's accounts;
a feather whispers to the stones.

While clouds convene to praise the dead,
tornadoes rant like oracles.
The roots are muttering, and the bones.

After Midnight

Last night the years surrounded me,
some bright as silver keys,
some like chords flickering in a dream.
The radio I slept by muttered jazz.
My clock glowed across the room,
its hands sweeping the seconds by,
the hours under,
the wind across the world.
Then Bird blew in,
blew back the clouds
that rained just yesterday,
and I heard that music of the spheres
the ancients heard.
I heard them blues
blown through a horn of stars.

• Addie Parker's Blues

I be here waiting
When my boy drags home.
He know where to find me
When he feeling like a stone.

Whose back room you shacked up in,
High on the sound of your horn?
What gal's wailing, "Baby,
Baby, for you I was born!?"

What game you playing, Baby,
Your Daddy didn't play?
Don't go balling with pretty Miss Bones
Or she roll you right away.

I hear them sirens crying down Troost,
Mr. Wheeler scuttling down the hall.
Woman, I asks myself, Woman,
Will your boy come home at all?

What game you playing, Baby,
Your Daddy didn't play?
Don't go balling with pretty Miss Bones
Or she roll you right away.

I be here waiting
When my boy drags home.
He know where to find me
When he feeling like a stone.

Black Woman, Enroute

Apart as old weather, across the aisle,
Locked in the seasons' slow erosion
Of stump teeth, numbed by the train's motion,
She looks across old distances, while
The car rattles and a sailor sways in his seat.
It's so easy to yawn, to turn away
From a black woman wrinkling in the heat,
Thumb through *Time* or savor *Woman's Day*.
But something sharper than words shivers on the page
As pieces of sooty landscape drop behind.
The train steams, stops. She jerks, clumsy with age,
Afraid she's lost, trying to find
A sign, some mark of place, something to show
She's on her way to where she wants to go.

Disillusionment at Dawn

At six o'clock their stirrings start:
Faucets squeak; windows creak and shut;
The risen sleepers paddle toward their afternoons.

The hour sets us moods apart:
I'm falling into darkness from my cot;
They reach for lights, for brushes, and for plastic brooms.

Outside my door, an hour ago,
Chilled by the morning and my journey home,
I watched the lamps washed out by dawn and drained of light.

They've just turned up the radio;
News and weather penetrate my room.
But I can't burrow deep enough, nor turn things right.

• *P. S.*

She emptied the closets of blouses, the house of perfume,
Packed her suitcase with colors, rushed for the plane,
Paused only for a moment, when she boarded,
Then turned and became another passenger,
Beyond his touch or call, already gone.
Around him people semaphored goodbyes,
Such anxious postscripts that he looked away.

He has ordered all deliveries stopped,
Cancelled *The Morning Express,* been eating out
In dim cafes. The house is an empty closet.
In places the flowered paper has begun to peel.
He teaches himself to rejoice at signs of decay.

◆ *At Dinner They Punned*

At dinner they punned, afterward drove silently.
At the station no time for them to stall,
Hardly even time to kiss properly.

Her white gloves flapped as the pullman steamed goodbye.
In moments she swept beyond recall,
And he was left with something in his eye.

New Year's Eve

The girl with the quick-silver eyes
    pricks her balloon and it pops!
      What's left of the year draining out
        but some pieces of string? The boys
          and their unsteady girls keep tilting the room.

Don't slip on the ice cubes coasting the floor;
    don't swallow too much of the bartender's bilge.
      Any second from out of the dark
        the waiter may bring in a plate full of war.

On U. S. 1

Hitchhiking south from Newark in the rain,
I taste the carbon furnaces in air.
Dump-fires smoke beside the road. Trucks strain
Up grade, plowing water, spurt down to where

Oil tanks squat like coffee tins between
The meadows and the Pennsylvania tracks;
Candle flames of amber twist and lean,
Trembling above the rows of chimney stacks.

We stop. Cops in slickers wave us by.
A tractor-trailer steams on the shoulder, wrecked,
Its windshield wipers moving slowly, slowly,
Like antennae of a dying insect.

Ninth Street Bar, Seen Through the Glass

These faces sip their siphoned dreams
Like minutes gathered drop by drop
From the backwash of memory.
And if the cornered moment seems
Too abstract, swaying, full, to stop,
They blame the gin or Bacardi.

They swim through a watercolor night,
Splash their talk along the bar,
Tropical fish in a gleaming tank
Set under a phosphorescent light;
And one, sluggish as a bloated gar,
Shivers in the shallows where he sank.

• *The Body of This World*

Was it sinus that kept Shakespeare up
Late in the London candlelight,
Or did Falstaff, swearing cup by cup
And banging on the walls all night?

What man's abstract when he blows his nose
Or scratches and sweats in the summer heat?
Ingenues squawk like crows,
Sometimes belch after they eat.

Even villains bellyache
When intrigue sours, begins to bore.
The heroes of our dreams awake,
Their covers scattered on the floor.

• *Biography*

For breakfast he sipped cider.
For lunch he ordered gin.
For dinner quaffed a highball;
his world still didn't spin.
The preacher remonstrated,
"Men drown themselves in sin."
But he just downed martinis
and outlived all his kin.

• *To Calypso: Five-Week-Old German Shepherd*

Calypso sleeps. For a moment we joke;
Operation Puddle's cancelled.
Later we'll stand omniscient,
Waiting for the pause and hover,
The telltale crouch. We play god;
She never seems to understand.
Last night, sometime between her yappings,
I dreamed we all were sniffing,
Aimlessly, innocent. The world
Was scattered with our droppings.
We frisked and chattered, when
Suddenly a Voice said, "No."
A Whirlwind pushed our noses into our mess.

• *A Matter of Balance*

Last night from a wing of a 747
I glanced down at the neon and the cars.
Far above Los Angeles I found
A highway between the asphalt and the stars.

The passengers all pointed out and gawked.
I did a handstand, made funny faces, too.
They never smiled, just covered up their eyes.
I guess they thought: Surely it can't be true.

We banked and turned. I didn't mind a bit
Except for the wind, which kept pulling my hair.
Though universal laws had let me be
I took that as a sign they still were there.

I leaned from the edge, washed my face in cloud.
Drenched in fog, I hardly even swayed.
I ignored the pressure building in my ears
Until we landed. Then I was afraid.

• *Excursion*

We drive inland together past the bogs,
along the sand banks where the pine trees grow
often no taller than boys on stilts. My girl,

asleep, jostles my arm as traffic clogs,
rubs me with her nose, then yawns, aglow
in passing lights. This borrowed car's a world

inside the world that's changing as we ride.
We hear no clang of bell buoys counting swells
that coil into waves, unroll upon the sand.

The mutter of engines muffles the mumbling tide.
But though we park among the peanut shells
and broken glass beside a root beer stand,

we are like divers in a bathysphere,
suspended in the underwater glow,
a pause somewhere between the land and sea.

Flickers of phosphorescent fish appear
as neon quivers. We check our maps and go,
drifting down midnight roads towards Bethany.

• *View from the Trestle*

When the pick hammers and the sledge beats
For the first time in the buffalo land
Where the sky silences exhaust sound

And a gold spike's driven in the ground
Of the great plains, enter a brass band,
Top hatted and silk scarfed. Kansas streets

And the clasped Colt will be the law now
As the railroaders in their drunk dawns,
Coin spent, shovels shouldered, roll down tracks.

Roots grow from even restlessness; shacks
Beside roadbed water tanks lure cows;
Where chickens peck gravel, farms sprout; towns

Poker by the rails as the chips pile
Into stovepipe and chimney. North, west,
South and east again, from Port Ludlow

To the Gulf, boxcars carry hobos,
Guns, and hothouse flowers, without rest,
Rumbling tons to stock the changing miles.

◆ *Lady in Waiting*

She would be there waiting, so they said,
eager for him, his body toned by flight,
his head full of cossack horses rearing.

Instead he found seamy strangers scheming
how to make the tight-thighed lady right.
They rushed the bloodshot immigrant to bed.

Once there he had to do it all alone,
mouth to mouth resuscitate the drowned,
soothe her pale bones, her too-blue lips,

kiss those delicate ears, fondle the tips
of her most intricate designs. Gowned
in a scarlet peignoir, at last she made sweet moan.

They lay there in a soothing afterglow
until the lady rose, dimly crossed the room,
pushed his window up, then laughed and laughed.

He shivered in the unexpected draft,
felt all her colors fading into gloom,
love squelched and nowhere else to go.

She slit his pockets, dismembered both his shoes,
with a grotesque giggle kicked his underwear
into the shadows underneath the bed.

It took awhile to drive her from his head,
to munch his roll, say he didn't care
She'd left him naked with nothing more to lose.

♦ *The Soviet Flu*

I lie here and wait
for something called health to arrive
like a pardon
or a visa.

Standing Before a Lit Menorah

Like scrolls inscribed along the Western Wall,
These letters of His changing name
Set the oldest message on the night:

Not simple joy, nor simply ritual,
Not proof of innocence or shame,
But our hardest hopes alive in this bristling light.

• *Learning About Easter and Passover*

"For one week and a day we eat no bread.
Stop fumbling, Son, and listen." I was eight.
"It won't be very long," my father said.
He told me more as well, but I was late
For ring-a-lievio and hardly heard.

The yard behind St. John's was where we played,
Squalling like starlings. Sometimes a nun came out
To hush us into quietness, dismayed
Less by our warrior hoots than by her doubt
Such wildness could in time be civilized.

Our armies scattered home at five o'clock;
Suppertime's the time to quit a war.
We fought one final skirmish down the block.
I made it up the steps. From the front door:
"See you tomorrow, Joey, Gang, so long!"

That Seder night my father told us all
About how once in Egypt we were slaves,
How God was good and answered Moses' call
And let us go by holding back the waves.
"Passover is the time to celebrate."

When I finished my wine I asked for more;
My father said to get drunk was a sin.
He sent me out to open up the door
To let the Spirit of Elijah in.
I heard the choir singing from St. John's.

The *matzo* we ate all through the holiday
Tasted like salted wafers, but more dry.
But when an eight-year-old rides out to play
He's got to chew on something besides sky.
I did next time I called Joey LaSalle.

I offered him some *matzo* and explained,
"It's Passover and we can't eat any bread."
He never tasted it but stared instead
As if remembering. "You killed our God," he blamed.

"How can you kill God?" I said.

• *Poem for a Bar Mitzvah**

My son has dreamed me dead
all over my right
to do with his life
what wisdom wills.
He'd bop my dictates with a Louisville slugger,
yank my level of diction down to asphalt,
stick a barb under my theoretical discourse.
He won't be fooled by language or logic
and he won't buy a soft sell from a hard old man.

He'll damn well climb his own shaky ladders,
fling bottles from garage roofs,
streak into the half-light
while my advice hardly stains his jeans.
Me, the rabbi, his grandfathers,
he's stuck us all limply in a vase
to gently wither out our days.
"But Pop," he said, "you're imagining it all;
I never said what you said I said."
Here we are again.

Yesterday, the air conditioner broken,
I yelled, "Get back here," to a pair of deaf sneakers.
He ran like a fox,
leaving me to sweat it out without a script,
to sulk in my Director's chair.

He explained to us later,
hugged us, said we were silly to worry,
brushed his teeth before bed.

He's on his way to his own sins,
so says the Law. It's about time:
My bingo board's loaded with his numbers.

*Many Jews believe that prior to the Bar Mitzvah the father assumes the son's sins. Afterward the son becomes fully responsible for his own behavior.

· *Survivor*

In the year of the plague
he watched the first born
herded into the river, wept
for the lost, for the scabby
children, for the paralytic,
for old women driven to madness
by memories trapped in their narrowing brains.

He devised names for the world,
curses sufficient for the boil
under the flesh, words
like broken chicken bones
stuck in the throat.

No matter what great weight
fell, he wriggled from under
the corner, floundered
ashore at the last, salt
pouring out of his ears.
His eyes pumped tears
as he feasted on remains.

In time he would sing
of survival, the cataracts
blurring pain, easing him
into fragrant asides, teaching
him a stiff calmness.
Nothing changes but what he sees.
He lies on a mat of prayer.

Yahrzeit

He lists them,
all the dead
ones he loved
& those they loved.
He lists them
on brown paper
bags to hang
in the sudden snow.

Like a scribe
he fashions their names,
weeping with each,
staining the crumpled bags.

It gives him pleasure
to think of them
shaking in April wind
like candleflames, warming
the early sprouts;
knowing his tears
will turn to dew.

◆ *The Holy Days*

the holy days are upon us
we need them
we must live with what we have been

the bank president
trembles in prayer
he is taking stock

we must live with him too

the salesman's wife
has dressed for the occasion
he wears a skullcap embroidered in silver
so he may be humble before God

they are loving parents

the holy days are upon us
dry in our mouths
as the dead we remember
the cantor teaches us to cry again
even in the Midwest

we need him
to keep our souls moist

• *The Tragedy of Shylock*

I

He fastens a frontlet of black between his eyes,
Twists round his arm seven loops of leather;
So phylacteried, in holy guise,
He prays in the corner of a curtained room,
Bending toward the east, his heels together.
Behind him Jessica scurries through the gloom.
She opens the shuttered window and leans out
Above the street, until the sailors shout,
"Look! Up there's the daughter of the Jew."

Shylock lays down his book and doffs his shawl,
Unwinds the binding from his bitten flesh.
His hands are soft, uncalloused by the awl,
Axe or hammer. He cannot farm nor fish,
Bear stones nor mix mortar, being a Jew,
He thinks, "My mind must be my instrument,
But it shall be as hard as any flint."

II

Already the Rialto's aclatter with trade.
He stops on the bridge to watch an auctioneer,
An exiled Genoese; the thief is paid
Five ducats for a scroll worth only two.
The mob loves open larceny it's clear,
But spits on the fairest contracts of a Jew.
Shylock slaps his thigh, then hurries straight
To where the messengers from Florence wait.
They carry news of his investments there.

Curses follow him. He does not reply.
Those wretches paw for ducats in the street,
Fawn round every nobleman that comes by,
Like greedy curs that yelp for scraps of meat.
He has none to waste. Let Antonio
Buy their love with coin. Meanwhile, Shylock
Will save and wait till famine comes, then mock.

III

By Christ, that bearded Jew goes by each day
While we Venetians sweat. We need new laws!
They say he keeps the customers away
By secret curses in his synagogue.
The state has gone to hell and he's the cause.
Look in his face. See you not the frog
Of evil there ready to croak with glee
At our despair? He wills our bankruptcy
As, even now, he strolls by the canal.

Crossing the open sewer of the town
Shylock pauses as rotten fruit floats by
And sludge-stained gondolas splash up and down.
He contemplates the water, then the sky:
Antonio has gambled and may lose.
Soon he may seek a loan. Let it be so.
Tomorrow may be his, more than they know.

IV

The sun hangs heavy in the humid air,
Like a melon overripe and soon to fall.
The smell of swollen fruit is everywhere.
Angry vendors shake their hats; the flies
Just circle and return. Beside a stall
Of grapes and apricots which neither buys,
Antonio, in his stylish cloak of green,
Ridicules Shylock's Jewish gabardine;
But merchants often scoff before they trade.

"No one but Shylock can furnish such a sum.
Three thousand ducats, Sir, is, as you say,
'Considerable', or you would never come
To Shylock. You'll have your loan without delay.
My only bond shall be a pound of flesh;
For since your presence here so honors me,
I pay you back with this absurdity."

V

Where is she now? I'll pamper her no more.
Nothing's been done. The beds are still unmade.
Spoiled child! What's this? A ducat on the floor?
I wonder: "Jessica, can you not hear?
In my own house must I be disobeyed?"
He shouts again. Still, she does not appear.
The sagging curtains stretch, brushed by the night.
He finds a candle. The draft blows out his light.
Slowly he turns the ducat in his hands.

The Gentiles taunt and catcall in the street.
I hope the fools learn soon their daughters play
To sailors' pipes! I'll find their sorrow sweet.
Yes, we are kinsmen in our hate, obey
The same necessities beyond our words.
Damn them! My daughter and my ducats gone,
My house is cleansed. My hatred presses on.

VI

Antonio has begged for a delay.
His ventures fail. This I could not foretell.
What use have I for ducats? He shall pay
The bond. My insult yields a dividend
That I'll not waste. I'll usher him to hell.
A hundred thousand ducats could not bend
My purpose now. Venetians, best beware,
My daughter sickened in your unclean air,
But Shylock sucks revenge and keeps his health.

They ask for Christian mercy from a Jew,
As if I cared for their philosophy.
If I just pulled his beard and then withdrew,
What would be gained? They'd not let Shylock be.
But when was mercy ever sired by hate?
When were mad dogs caressed? Let them learn this:
Good begets good; evil begets justice.

VII

I've been betrayed. I planned to use their laws
To drain some poison from my festering hate.
Instead, a deft Delilah wins applause.
Their learned phrases, robes, and courtly mien
Bespoke some principle. But all was bait
And Shylock bit. I'll not do so again.
Decrees be damned! My bond shall still come due.
Though I am baptised, I am still a Jew.
They'll find this counterfeit less dyed than stained.

* * *

Whom shall I will my ducats? Christian and Jew
Despise me now with cause. That I were stone
And could forget! My spittle chokes. I chew
My own insides. My anger scrapes the bone.

Their holy water drowned me in my hate.
I am uncleansed who had been cleansed before.
My place in heaven's taken by a whore.

Wedding at the Western Wall

Behind their silhouetted kiss
Shadows are ciphered in the stone.
Must they be frightened knowing this?
Lovers have never loved alone.

• *Things Always Need Repairing*

After the tickle of rice and
The motorcade of horns, they learn
Things always need repairing.
They can't hammer long
And stay simple and dreaming.
The years flake off their roof,
And the seasons like downspouts
Twist awry. The payments dwindle
And, quiet as rust, they grow old.

• *A Monument of Feeling Stones*

For Rose Jaffe

She hovered beneath a half-familiar blur
Of children's voices, her sons and grandsons.
Like a monument of feeling stones, we ringed
Her bed, knowing not how to cry or not
To cry, flailing each other with glances, aware
Our own deaths circled in the room.
We stroked her hair, fine as a child's, caressed
Her infant-wizened face with fingertips
Sensitive as cilia. Her eyes,
Pale as overcast moons, eased downwards,
And we floated on the surface of her sleep.

• *Leaving Murray Hall, Elizabeth, N.J.*

Grandpa bequeathed the house
to all his children equally.
Equally they squeezed their arteries
and looked out and away.
They would not see the cracked tiles,
the splintered, dried out railings,
the nearly worn through rugs
they had worn down, sons and daughters
growing into America. They would not
though they could. Each
questioned each for not repairing
what he could not admit had gone
beyond repair. Finally, the Irish realtor
sold their inheritance
to five Franciscan priests
who still preferred the Mass in Latin.

For the sons, the daughters, the grandchildren,
there is no going home to Murray Hall.
No mezuzah grips the doorpost. At sundown
no prayers murmur from the southeast corner.
I can no longer drink glasses of tea
in that kitchen, no longer quarrel over books
surrounded by crumbs on Grandpa's table.
I almost cannot speak.

• *Menorah Hospital, May 30, 1971, 9:55 a.m.*

Anna Gabrielle,
    your mama, holding her breath,
    shoved you out into the morning
    with four stunning pushes
    her smile an arc of sunlight
    splashing my face
    as you cried hello to the already world.
    Then she called out softly:
        My grandmother died in this hospital.
        Her name was Anna
            and I loved her.
        But, Death,
            now I'm even.

*Waiting for You to Reappear
In the House We Never Left*

I told our disastrously beautiful daughter
to wipe up the dog food in the back hall,
and with a damp paper towel she collected flecks
of her father's anger.
Not knowing what she had,
she tossed them into the trash
on top of an old poem
nestled in the folds of a diaper.

You and I were not there.
We are not in this house any more.
We have been left somewhere,
bits and pieces in envelopes
sent out into the world with checks
labeled VISA or Bell Tel.
There is a woman with your name hereabouts,
but I do not know her.
You live in photographs
and in my memory give me solace.
I have tried to track you down,
thought at times you were out back
or upstairs or doing laundry,

that I would catch your smile
on the tip of my tongue.
But it was someone else.
I try to think of other things:
Of Anna's jet lashes,
of Michael's solid bass-player hands,
of Marina's spontaneous song.
Once I start
I can't leave any of them out.
Tamar, let me comb the snags from your hair.
Hang on, Jonathan, hug your father's neck.
And Sara, first daughter of my life,
let us take long walks together and talk of Jerusalem.

My Grandpa and his father look down at me
from the walls of this house
my father helped us buy.
What do I say to them?
What do I ask?

I sit in a flowered chair
snatched from a Goodwill store in better times
and weep for the dead I love
who would weep for me if they could.
The things around me,
shells, clocks, books, and chairs,
are full of the past,
and I am full of the present
which makes everything fade.

But I cannot sit here long.
I hear the back door.
Maybe it's you.
Maybe I will catch you beside the refrigerator
before you can change or hide.
Maybe you will tell me where you have been.

• *The Year We Moved from Currey Head*

for Sam Jaffe

When Skippy strangled one April afternoon,
My mother whimpered and my father cursed.
They wouldn't let me have another dog.
I cried for the dog they wouldn't let me have.

When I was ten I already knew
The absence death is. No logic told me,
I knew her voice was not just silent
But was stilled. Father finally spoke,
"Your mother's gone away. She won't be back."
I cried for my mother who had gone away.

That year we moved from Currey Head,
On a Sunday morning pendulous with bells.
We didn't wave, just drove away,
Forgetting nothing that we meant to take
But taking much I know we should have left;

Behind us on the steps of Sacred Heart
Mother's Catholic friends, like an April garden,
Waited in flowered hats for noonday Mass,
When all at once it rained. As I looked back
I saw them scatter and umbrellas blossom.

We drove 'cross town through rain. Each time we stopped
My father blew his nose. At Grandpa's house,
All of us, with cartons in our arms,
Climbed upstairs to the plaster-boarded rooms
That seemed to tremble when my father snored.
Mornings, to wake me up for school,
Grandma would pound her ceiling with a broom.

The backyard grapes bulged in the sun, and squirrels
Frisked along the drains while Grandma baked.
She let me lick the mixing spoon and bowl
To celebrate another birthday cake.
(At dinner no one mentioned it had burned.)
I asked how old my father was. They laughed
When I told them what they told me was a lie.
I spoiled their party then and slammed the door.

Later, I called downstairs to say goodnight,
But they were gone, Grandma and Grandpa to bed,
My father out. I lay and watched the leaves
Shuddering on the ceiling of my room,
Then fell asleep. Afterward I woke
And listened for my father's snores but heard
Only the crickets and the scuffling of the leaves.

I waited at my window, watching cars;
They all turned off our street or passed the house.
The trees were full and shadows of their leaves
Swam in the puddle of the streetlamp's light.

Then, finally, footsteps halfway down the block.
Then louder on the sidewalk out in front.
I listened for my father at the door,
But then I heard the footsteps farther on.

I cried for father to come home again.
I was too much a part of that coming and going
To grant some stranger had just happened by.
I listened for the footsteps coming back;
All the stirs of night were steps returning,
Till, weary from so much imagined walking,
I almost slept, my head against the pane.
Once, I thought I heard my father's breathing,
But it was just the shuffling of the leaves.

There, in that narrow room of nervous shadows,
That sudden image of my father paled,
And, when I cried for father to come home,
All my senses shuddered like the leaves.

· *The Middle Aged Man Looks Out into the Gulf*

He listens to himself
like a man taking his own blood pressure.

If he knew the currents,
how he would drift,
he would let loose.

But getting old is more than sailing further,
requires more than ancient craft.
The tried tactics put off nothing.

He thinks if he knew more
he would flinch less.

Sometimes he looks at those
who have gone even further,
and he vows to write letters
to his own future, to tell himself
what he will need to know.

He wonders if he is really going
forward or backward to confusion
only with new clarity.

Questions curl around him like theories.
He would snatch something more
from the uncertain journey
than a single tic of insight.

He would snatch more than a moment
of love or language,
more than one deep breath.

He aches for a lengthening
curve of meaning that turns
back on itself again and again
like a radiant wave.

• *Breathing In*

He is no ordinary fisherman,
One who knows about lures and leader.
Chance more than maps brought him to this pond.
Under a willow he lets his line haphazardly drift.
Light crinkles the water and his cork trembles.
He waits for nothing to bite.
What is he doing here at dawn
But breathing in the universe,
Letting the tadpole and the bullfrog happen?
His pole bends as if to question,
And his line grows taut, luminous with drops.
Up from under, browner than age,
The prehistoric catfish, like a bearded reply,
Tugs at the sun.

• *They Would Be My Poems*

Down with the flu
I read Amichai.
I call out to my wife
and my son
to read with me
and weep together.

If I were a Jew in Jerusalem,
older than I am, by eleven years,
if I were not of this time,
not of this place,
Yehuda, they would be my poems.

As it is, I steal them.
Like an old man in the ghetto market
I pick them up and drop them
into the linings of my heart.

◆ Whitman on a Scaffold

The old man leans over the world,
over the tiger lilies growling against stones,
over clotheslines twitching in the wind,
over sunflowers statuesque as sculpture.
Paint streaks his jeans, cerulean and ocean green.
He is an odd flower perched there, a smatter of color,
dipping the rooftops with the texture of clouds.
We rub our eyes and do not believe him.
He is a figment of architecture lit by the sun
to dazzle us to madness.
"Show us!" we cry, here in "flashing Missouri,"
but we dare not trust our eyes.

But over our shoulders, from behind our curtains,
in the tilted rearview mirrors of our Fords and Chevies,
we notice him again, ask what the hell he's doing up there.
He has taken a break for an afternoon guzzle in the sun.
His fingertips red with wine, he stretches,
for a man at work, indecently. From his side
he slips an antique spyglass. Casually
he wets the folds of his lips with his tongue,
sways there on the scaffold, his hips rocking.
As the beams collect the telescope expands,

his eyes grow sensuous. He is looking at us!
Voyeur on a scaffold, who sees too much,
who must stroke with each look
even the capillaries, know the intimacy
of the most secret blush.

How he must hurt on his scaffold there,
obsessed by seeing all, by seeing all:
    the pimp kicking the pricked prostitute,
    the child crying behind the garage,
    the jagged scar under the makeup,
    treacherous limbs and lush embraces,
    handclasps and forked fingers,
    the hungry and the squanderers, all
    who climb up the beams
    to slide inside his eyes.

He forgets nothing; not the sure glint of the aluminum siding
or the delicacy of affection. Of it all
he will make singing, perilous on his scaffold,
daring to waver on edges, to risk
sudden angular gestures, to lurch
himself over space

and pull back, to juggle
wisps and chips, locks and letters,
mothballs and maiden hairs.
He motions that he will descend,
that he will lie down like the cat
under the stoop, that he will finger
minutia, tease all to life again.
But already we have turned the corner toward darkness
and the angle is wrong for seeing
the probe of his glass
the flambeau that curls from his chin.
But if we should rocket outward,
forgetting farewells,
not even waving like the last lingering grasses,
far out among the stars
one of us will surely notice
across a porthole of our spaceship
a miraculous strand of beard.

· *Round for One Voice*

I tried to make a world inside a poem,
Stocked it with kites cavorting in the sun,
With windblown leaves on shadowed window sills,
With showers speckling a pond by a greening field,
With the laughter of geese and the slow solemnity of cows.
Such genesis was the least of miracles:
Why here's a sun, its atoms writhing, and here
A moon, tilted like a rocking chair.
I plant some hills and watch the mountains grow,
Irrigate a desert with my words.

But how can I name the shapes I have imagined,
Pin down each speck under the whirling sky?
Bulls snort in fields beside the trembling cows;
Rain floods the ponds; soil slides from treeless hills.
On Ararat a snake waits for the dove.
Though ancient storms on the sun besiege the eye
And men learn Hell's a crater on the moon,
I try to make a poem inside the world.

• Acknowledgments are due to the following publications in which some of these poems have appeared:

• *Focus Midwest*; *Jewish Currents*; *Sunday Clothes*; *Prairie Schooner*; *Saturday Review*; *Kansas City Star*; *Harrison Street Review*; *The Salt Creek Reader*; *News Letters*; *Ladies Home Journal*; *New York Times*; *Kansas City Jewish Life*; *Dacotah Territory, a 10 year Anthology* (North Dakota Institute for Regional Studies); *Patterns of Poetry: An Encyclopedia of Forms* (Louisiana State University Press); *Together Let's Prepare* (Childbirth Education Assocation); *How To Eat a Poem* (Missouri Arts Council); *Voices Within the Ark* (Avon); *Fathers* (Dacotah Territory Press); *Voices from the Interior* (BkMk Press, UMKC); *The Muscles and the Bones That Carry Us to Love* (Walton Music Co.).

• "View from the Trestle" was part of a concert chorale, *A Lesson in Geography,* performed under the auspices of the National Endowment for the Arts and the Mid-America Arts Alliance.